Original title:
Flora and Flair

Copyright © 2025 Creative Arts Management OÜ
All rights reserved.

Author: Nathaniel Blackwood
ISBN HARDBACK: 978-1-80566-739-1
ISBN PAPERBACK: 978-1-80566-868-8

The Elegance of Eco

In a world where plants wear shoes,
The daisies dance in bright red hues.
A cactus tries to wear a hat,
While bunnies laugh, 'What's up with that?'

Trees gossip 'bout the latest trends,
Squirrels sport the newest bends.
The flowers prank the passing bees,
Swapping nectar with a sneeze!

The Garden of Radiance

In this garden, all's a joke,
Roses giggle, not a poke.
Tulips wear their polka dots,
While sunflowers play tic-tac-toe spots.

Worms offer fashion tips so bold,
"Dress in mud, it never gets old!"
The lilies laugh in leafy dreams,
Turning up their bloom with screams!

Lullabies in Lavender

Underneath the lavender skies,
Crickets sing with quirky sighs.
A firefly plays piano bright,
While frogs take turns in a dance at night.

A butterfly whispers, 'Take a nap!'
While ants prepare a snack, a trap!
The moon rolls in, a sleepy light,
And in this chaos, all feels right.

Petals in the Wind

Petals twirl like dizzy spies,
As dandelions tell their lies.
"Skydiving's fun!" says the sweet rose,
While violets giggle from their toes.

The breeze brings laughter, twirls in flight,
As petals play hide-and-seek at night.
"Don't you dare land on my spot!"
The charming blooms give all they've got!

Symphonic Stems

In a garden where tulips dance,
They twirl and sway, given a chance.
Daisies gossip, very absurd,
While sunflowers sing, quite undeterred.

Bees wear hats, with swagger so grand,
Bopping to rhythms, a floral band.
Roses laugh, with petals so bright,
Telling jokes under soft moonlight.

Secret Garden Chronicles

A secret place where carrots laugh,
Talking veggies, what a gaffe!
Radishes tease, with roots so deep,
While cabbage dreams of a far-off sweep.

Chillies prance with fiery glee,
While pumpkins giggle beneath the tree.
The garlic whispers, so pungent and sly,
"Did you hear what the potatoes replied?"

The Palette of Twilight

Colors burst as dusk unfolds,
Petunias gossip, secrets told.
Lavenders sigh with fragrant flair,
While night blooms chuckle, unaware.

Snapdragons snap, their jaws in play,
Petals flutter, a bright ballet.
As dusk paints dreams, so vividly,
The nightshade winks, mischievously.

Whimsy in the Weeds

Among the weeds, a party's found,
With dandelions dancing all around.
A clover juggles, quite the show,
While thistles grin, all aglow.

The motley crew of green and gold,
Share wisecracks that never get old.
In laughter, they sway with glee,
Nature's jesters, wild and free.

Nature's Color Palette

In the garden, colors dance,
Red like a clumsy romance.
Yellow blooms with a goofy twist,
Bluebell giggles, can't resist.

Sunflowers wear hats so tall,
While daisies trip and gently fall.
Green leaves gossip in the breeze,
Whispering secrets with such ease.

Lilies take a selfie spree,
Roses laugh, 'Look at me, see?'
Petal parties with wild cheer,
Nature's fun is crystal clear.

Violets paint the grass with flair,
Mismatched colors, everywhere.
In this patch of pure delight,
Laughter echoes day and night.

Blooming Reverie

A daffodil's a little clown,
Wearing sunshine, upside down.
Tulips gossip over tea,
Swapping stories joyfully.

Peonies prance in the breeze,
Swaying to their own sweet tease.
Carnations say, 'Check my pose!'
While marigolds strike silly prose.

Zinnias boast about their bling,
'Look at these petals, aren't we kings?'
Dandelions float with grace,
Offering wishes in a race.

In a meadow filled with cheer,
Every bloom has jokes to share.
Nature's laughter fills the air,
A blooming day, beyond compare.

A Symphony of Stems

The tulips tap a little beat,
While daisies dance with tiny feet.
Cactus tries to join the fun,
But gets tangled; oh what a run!

Roses play a jig so fine,
Orchids groove in a dainty line.
Sunflowers twirl, a grand recital,
Pansies giggle, love the vitals.

Lilies hum their softest tune,
Bouncing high, they touch the moon.
In this garden, music swells,
Every stem a story tells.

Petals clap and cheer aloud,
A symphony that's nature-proud.
Join the dance, don't be a bore,
In this concert, there's always more!

The Language of Blooms

A sunflower says, 'You're so bright!'
A lilac winks, 'What a delight!'
Petunias chat with pure delight,
While violets plot a playful fight.

Roses blush with every tease,
Buds whisper secrets 'neath the trees.
Daisy chains and laughter rings,
The garden blooms with funny things.

A dandelion blows a kiss,
Floating seeds, a child's wish.
Bramble bush wears prickly shoes,
Dance with thorns, can't refuse!

Nature's blooms unlock a grin,
In a world where we all win.
Every flower speaks its part,
With a giggle from the heart.

Nectar's Story

In a garden bright, bees start to sway,
Sipping sweet juice, they dance away.
Blossoms giggle, petals spry,
'What's for lunch?' they ask, oh my!

On a sunflower, a bee takes a peek,
'What's the buzz?' he starts to speak.
'With pollen art, we're here to play,
Turn the drab into a cabaret!'

Daisies drop jokes, a riot in bloom,
While roses blush, creating a room.
'Laughter, dear weeds, is our great mission,
Snapping selfies, we've got ambition!'

As butterflies prance with style so great,
They slip on petals, it's never too late.
Nectar's sweet story, a comic delight,
In this wild garden, we party all night!

A Harvest of Hues

A stroll through the patch, what a sight!
Painted in colors, oh, pure delight!
Carrots wear hats, all tall and green,
Radishes giggle, 'We're the best seen!'

Tomatoes do tango, ripe to the core,
While zucchinis chat, 'We're never a bore!'
'Watch out for veggies who think they can dance,
We twist and we shout, not leaving to chance!'

Sunflowers boasting, heads held so high,
They wink at the cabbages passing by.
'Let's throw a bash, we'll bring out the stew,
With laughs and a harvest as bright as the dew!'

In this patch of joy, who'll steal the show?
Every leaf and stem, it's a musical flow.
With laughter and colors that sprout and entwine,
Join hands with the greens, sip water and wine!

Poppy Whispers

In a field of poppies, whispers arise,
'These dresses we wear are a great surprise!'
Red, pink, and orange, all twirling about,
'We're the fashion stars, without a doubt!'

Ladybugs listen, on this stylish spree,
'Which pattern's the best? Come and see!'
Poppies giggle, caught in the breeze,
'We're all runway models, aiming to please!'

But a strong wind comes, and they start to sway,
'Careful now, don't blow us away!'
With laughter and color, they dance in the sun,
Each petal a joke, oh, what joyous fun!

So they twirl and they giggle, in shades bold and bright,
Poppy whispers carry, from morning till night.
'What will we wear? More colors to share!'
'Just be yourself, my dears, that's the flair!'

Couplet of Carnations

Carnations gather for a grand old chat,
'Who wore it best? Oh, imagine that!'
With ruffles and frills, all sewn with care,
'It's our day to shine, let's take to the air!'

One petal quipped, 'I've got a new style!'
The others erupted in giggles and smiles.
'Twist me to the left, then spin like a dream,
In this fashion parade, we're bursting at the seam!'

They twirl and they whirl, a colorful dance,
Mixing their shades, oh! What a chance!
With laughter and flair, they brighten the scene,
'Join us, dear daisies, let's form a routine!'

As the night settles, it's time for a song,
Carnations unite, nothing feels wrong.
In this joyful bunch, with humor so rare,
Together they laugh, creating a fair!

Nature's Immaculate Palette

A redflower whispers, "Don't be shy!"
While bluebells giggle as they sway by.
The daisies argue who's the brightest here,
While sunflowers turn to the cheerful cheer.

In shadows, greens plot a sneaky scheme,
Yellow blooms grin, chasing the dream.
Roses blush with a flirty tease,
While the violets laugh in the gentle breeze.

Threads of Terrestrial Elegance

A dandy dandelion, quite the show,
Waves at every breeze and steals the glow.
With twirly stalks, the plants commence,
To sway and gossip, it's pure suspense.

A thistle pricks the daisies' delight,
While roses pout, feeling not quite right.
They strut their stuff in a lively ballet,
And bees chuckle as they buzz on their way.

The Wild Elegance of Vines

Vines are tangled in a playful knot,
Dancing around with the charm they've got.
They giggle softly in the moonlit night,
While lanterns of fireflies join the delight.

With leafy hair, they twist and twirl,
Inviting the stars for a ridiculous whirl.
One brave vine tried to climb a fence,
But waved goodbye and fell with suspense.

Petal Poise

Petals parade in a colorful line,
Each one boasting, "Oh, I'm divine!"
Lilies wink with a graceful charm,
While orchids giggle, "Who needs alarm?"

The tulips blush at the sight of the sun,
In full bloom, they race for fun.
With a gentle nudge, they all start to dance,
While bumblebees buzz and take a chance.

Dance of the Daisies

Daisies spinning with glee,
Stomping feet but can't you see?
Wiggly stems, they jig and sway,
Digging holes, then falling prey.

Petals laugh, they pat the ground,
Tickled by the winds around.
A bumblebee joins in the fun,
Buzzing loud, 'I'm number one!'

Butterflies wing in with flair,
Whispering secrets, they love to share.
'What's the gossip?' one asks near,
'Oh, the frogs? They dance in cheer!'

The sun sets low, the show is grand,
A daisy twirls, takes a stand.
With all their friends, they'll spin and prance,
Into the night, they take a chance.

Echoes of Wildflowers

In the meadow, wild and free,
Flowers gossip about the bee.
'I heard he's quite the hotshot now,'
'Always buzzing, take a bow!'

Roses poke their thorns in jest,
'You know we're simply the best!'
Wildflowers blink with cheeky grins,
'We'll outshine you with our spins!'

Dandelions play hide and seek,
Puffing out their seeds with cheek.
'Catch me if you think you can,'
As seeds float off like a plan.

But when the rain begins to fall,
They huddle close, a floral ball.
Echoes of laughter fill the air,
As petals dance without a care.

The Velvet Canopy

Underneath the leafy dome,
Nature's laughter feels like home.
Squirrels prance in velvety suits,
Making mischief with their hoots.

Mushrooms wearing polka dots,
Wave their caps in funny spots.
Toadstools giggle, 'Join the line!'
'We're having fun, won't you be mine?'

The sun peeks through, a playful spy,
Whispering jokes to passersby.
Roots chuckle, 'What's with the fuss?'
While vines entangle in a rush.

As twilight falls, they sing a tune,
A chorus beneath the silver moon.
With every leaf, a secret shared,
In this canopy, all souls are paired.

Fragrant Dreams

A lavender cloud floats by,
Whiffs of dreams that make you sigh.
Petunias in silly hats parade,
'It's a fashion show!' they loudly brayed.

Pansies wink with playful charms,
'We're the cuties here on farms!'
Sunflowers tower with heads held high,
'Pose for the camera, oh my, oh my!'

Daffodils giggle, twirling around,
In this garden, joy is found.
Colors splash like vibrant cream,
Sprinkling fun in every dream.

As the dusk creeps gently near,
They whisper secrets, loud and clear.
In fragrant fields where laughter plays,
Joy sprouts up in delightful ways.

Whirlwinds of Wildflowers

In a field where daisies dance,
A bee took quite a chance.
He zoomed in for a golden snack,
Bumped a bug, and off it flack!

The tulips giggled, swayed with ease,
While clovers chuckled in the breeze.
The sunflowers waved, tilting heads,
As bumblebees took cozy beds.

A dandelion, full of fluff,
Whispered secrets, though a bit tough.
"Let's start a party, wild and bright,
With fruit punch made from morning light!"

So petals painted, colors bright,
In this bloom brawl, a hilarious sight.
Each flower grinned, no worries here,
In gusts of laughter, all held dear.

Elysian Fields of Flora

In fields where petals dance and play,
A squirrel joined the flower ballet.
He slipped on blooms, went round and round,
Creating chaos on the ground!

A ladybug, dressed in polka dots,
Tried to solve a puzzle with knots.
"Why am I here? What's my role?
To cheer or just to eat a shoal?"

The sun tossed rays like confetti,
As grasshoppers cheered, bright, and petty.
With a flip and a hop, they took a stance,
Turning the meadow into a dance!

In this playful realm, quite absurd,
Even the roots had laughter stirred.
With giggles echoing through the air,
Joy sprung wildly everywhere!

Celestial Blooms

In gardens where the stardust glows,
A flower proudly strikes a pose.
"Look at me, I'm quite divine!"
Said the pink petal, sipping wine!

The violets giggled, chin up high,
"Shimmer, shimmer, we touch the sky!"
With unicorns prancing by their side,
Each petal flaunted with such pride.

An orb-weaver spun tales of glee,
"I'm the web weaver, watch and see!"
But tripped on a twig, fell on his back,
And in that moment, all senses lack!

With cacti laughing, quite beside,
They formed a club, their joy amplified.
In a whirl of petals, gleeful bloom,
Where laughter bloomed, like sweet perfume!

The Canvas of Growth

On a canvas where plants collide,
A witty vine began to glide.
"Look at my twist, what a great art!"
While daisies burst out, "Oh, you're so smart!"

But vines got tangled, what a sight!
They argued fiercely day and night.
"You're just a weed, and I'm the star!"
Replied the sun, shining from afar.

The carrots chuckled in their rows,
"Why all this fuss over who grows?"
"Let's take a sip of morning dew,
And paint the world with joy anew!"

In this garden of jests and spray,
Life's the canvas, come what may!
With laughter echoing through the green,
They painted fun, in every scene!

Secrets Under the Canopy

In the shade of leafy trees,
A squirrel plots with utmost ease.
He lost his acorn in a race,
Now he's got a nutty face!

When birds gossip, they squeak and squawk,
About the rabbit's silly walk.
The daisies dance, they twirl and sway,
While ants march on a picnic tray!

A hedgehog snores, well, that's his jam,
Dreaming of cheese and buttered ham.
Underneath the sky so grand,
The forest laughs, it's a jolly band!

So come and sit beneath the shade,
Where every secret is displayed.
Laugh with friends, forget your woes,
In this green world where humor grows!

Caprice of the Chrysanthemum

Oh, the chrysanthemum's a charmer,
With petals soft and wild as karma.
It sways too bold, it swings too fine,
    It thinks it's truly divine!

When clouds roll in, it turns and frowns,
    Donning a gown of leafy crowns.
But when the sun comes out to play,
    It giggles in a sunny sway!

A bee buzzes past, a bit bemused,
"Why wear a tutu? You're confused!"
Yet still the flower just prances on,
In pink and yellow, dusk till dawn!

So next time you see that bloom so bright,
Remember its dance, its sheer delight.
For in its heart, a laugh's in bloom,
Creating joy 'neath the sky's big room!

The Sway of the Sunflowers

Sunflowers stretch, they reach for gold,
With necks that wobble, oh so bold.
They wink at bees, they twist and twirl,
As if to say, "Oh boy, let's whirl!"

A bumblebee hops from one to two,
"It's pollen party! Who's dancing too?"
With all that buzzing, who needs a beat?
These blooms really know how to move their feet!

When the wind blows, it's quite the sight,
They sway and bow with all their might.
A big bright family, so full of cheer,
Drawing in laughter, year after year!

So if you stroll through fields of sun,
Just join the party, it's so much fun!
With every sway, they'll make you grin,
In a land where the dance will never thin!

Pollen and Poetry

Under the sky, where flowers conspire,
Pollen drifts like poetic fire.
The daisies write verses in the breeze,
A spunky tale to tickle knees!

A honeybee hums a silly tune,
As violets giggle by the moon.
"Let's pen a sonnet about our plight,
Of chasing sunbeams, oh what a sight!"

The lavender ponders, with a nod,
"Let's mention bees who often plod.
With tiny feet and fuzzy hats,
Creating honey, imagine that!"

So gather 'round and hear the tale,
Of flowers, bees, and all that grail.
In pollen's embrace, let's all decree,
Life's a poem, wild and free!

Petals in the Breeze

The daisies danced with glee,
As bumblebees buzzed around.
One slipped on a petal,
And tumbled to the ground.

Lilies laughed, oh so loud,
As they swayed in the sun.
A squirrel joined the party,
Now everyone's having fun!

Tulips wore shades so cool,
Looking sharp, oh what a sight!
A playful breeze swirled in,
Turning day into night.

With petals in the air,
Joyful chaos does reign.
Nature's silly circus,
A true delight with no pain.

Whispers of the Garden

In the garden, secrets spread,
As flowers plot and scheme.
A rose tells a joke,
While the marigold beams.

Tulips gossip in hush,
About the daisies' dress.
'Too bright!' they all giggle,
'Oh, what a mess!'

Still, sunflowers stand tall,
Grinning at the fuss.
'Don't mind the laughter,
It's just the wind's trust!'

Even the weeds join in,
With a chuckle and cheer.
In this garden of whispers,
Laughter's the main frontier.

Blossoms in the Moonlight

When the moon takes the stage,
The blossoms start to sway.
Petals giggle softly,
In a magical ballet.

A nightingale croons tunes,
To entertain the dew.
A flower wriggles in time,
With a pirouette or two.

The jasmine starts to snicker,
At the tulip's clumsy twist.
All under silver beams,
How could they resist?

Each blossom shines so bright,
While fireflies play the fool.
In the moonlit garden,
Every night's a riotous school.

The Secret Life of Leaves

Leaves chatter on the trees,
In a whimsical debate.
'Are we hats for birds?'
Or 'Can we do a crate?'

One leaf fancied a sail,
Another dreamed of flight.
They giggled at their dreams,
Under the starry night.

Some leaves tried to play catch,
But went whirling past the sun.
While others basked in shade,
Claiming victory, just for fun!

Oh, the secrets that they share,
While fluttering on the breeze.
In a world so full of green,
Life's a ticklish tease!

The Glimmer of Green

In a garden so bright, things bloom with delight,
A squash in a hat, looks ready for flight.
Daisies wear glasses, they laugh and they cheer,
While tomatoes dance, bringing everyone near.

The lettuce is gossiping, full of good news,
While onions cry, but they're hiding their blues.
Sunflowers twirl in a waltz of their own,
While the carrots are busy, chilling in their throne.

Bumblebees buzzing, they're plotting a show,
With petals for curtains, putting on a glow.
A radish in clown shoes, it squeaks with a grin,
The fun never stops when nature's in spin.

So join in the laughter, let your heart sing,
In this lively place, where joy is the king.
With every green leaf, there's a story to tell,
In the garden of chuckles, everything's swell.

Dreaming in the Petal Patch

In the patch where flowers grew tall and proud,
A daffodil whispered secrets out loud.
The tulips wore hats and shoes made of lace,
While daisies formed a conga line in the space.

Bumblebees buzzed in a wacky parade,
With sunflowers leading, it was quite the charade.
Butterflies' wings, they shimmered like gold,
In a whimsical world, a joy manifold.

The wind played a tune, a jazzy old riff,
The daisies responded with a delicate shift.
A rose struck a pose, with flair and a twist,
In a dreamlike dance, you just couldn't resist.

With laughter and petals, the night danced away,
In a whimsical patch where the flowers play.
So if you feel down, take a stroll through the blooms,
And let all your worries dissolve in the fumes.

Petals and Paintbrushes

With brushes in hand, we paint the scene bright,
Where petals have colors that dance in the light.
Each stroke brings a chuckle, each hue brings a cheer,
As blossoms enlist in the art that is near.

The roses are blushing, giggling in pink,
While violets whisper as if they can think.
A peony posed, trying hard to look fine,
While daisies just laughed, sipping dew like wine.

The canvas of nature is splashed with delight,
As blooms take their turns, it's a festival night.
Even weeds join the fun, in polka dot glee,
Creating a chaos of color and spree.

With laughter and joy, in the garden they sway,
These artists of nature paint magic each day.
So grab your own brush, let your colors unfurl,
In a patch of hilarity, let your heart swirl.

The Veins of the Earth

Underneath the soil lies a giggling web,
Worms sing a chorus, they're quite the celeb.
The roots hold a meeting, discussing their dreams,
While rocks roll their eyes, plotting mischievous schemes.

Mushrooms don hats and throw parties with flair,
With the mushrooms' confetti filling the air.
The daisies peek down, curious and spry,
As the earthworms throw dances, reaching for the sky.

The stones share their wisdom, what they've learned well,

From ages of dreams in their earthen-shell.
Each layer of soil, a story unfolds,
In the belly of nature, where laughter beholds.

So if you should wander where the green roots entwine,
Listen close for the giggles, they're truly divine.
In the veins of the ground, there's a jolly old sound,
Of the earth's cheeky laughter, forever unbound.

Moments in the Meadow

In a meadow where daisies laugh,
A butterfly danced, what a gaffe!
It tripped on its wings, oh so bright,
Flew into a flower, what a sight!

The bees had a party, honey in hand,
They spoke of their plans to form a band.
With buzzing and giggles, they swayed and twirled,
A chorus of chaos in this bright world.

A rabbit played hopscotch, daring and bold,
It tripped on a clover, the story is told.
With carrots as prizes for winning the race,
They all joined in laughter, what a wild chase!

As the sun dipped low, and shadows did roam,
The flowers all whispered, "Let's go home!"
With petals a-fluttering, a soirée concluded,
In this meadow of mischief, joy never eluded!

Garden of Forgotten Whispers

In the garden of lost and found,
A snail wore a hat, looking quite profound.
It said to a beetle, "What's new today?"
The beetle just laughed, then rolled away.

A gnome took a selfie, posed by the rose,
Its face turned blue, he forgot to say cheese!
The flowers were giggling, petals in glee,
As the gnome sat down, stuck in a tree.

A scarecrow danced with the wind in the eve,
With ribbons and daisies, it spun to believe.
The crows thought it funny, a sight so bizarre,
To see such a figure, both twisted andjar.

The night crept in softly, stars gave a wink,
As shadows began to dance, and flowers would blink.
In whispers of jasmine, secrets did flow,
In this garden of giggles, laughter would grow!

Petals and Personality

A sunflower swaggered, all tall and grand,
Telling tall tales of the sun-warmed land.
"I'm the brightest around!" it bellowed with cheer,
But daisies just snickered, "Oh dear, oh dear!"

A tulip was prancing, wearing a shoe,
It twirled and it giggled, joined by a crew.
"These petals are fancy!" it flaunted with flair,
While grasshoppers chuckled, "What a stylish affair!"

A bumblebee buzzed, on a quest for sweet treats,
But tripped on a petal and landed in beats.
With flowers all laughing, they formed a new beat,
Their floral jubilee danced to the heat.

As twilight approached with stars shining bright,
The blooms gathered round, in pure delight.
With jokes and with jests, they shared with finesse,
In a garden of whimsy, there's joy to express!

Twinings of Thorns

In a cluster of thorns, a rose lost its flair,
While shouting at weeds, "Do I look like I care?"
The thorns wrapped around, a comical scene,
While daisies just giggled, "Oh, what a queen!"

A bramble spoke loudly, "I'm the best at a joke!"
It tickled the petals, and that's how it broke.
With laughter exploding, the thorns they forgot,
Swaying in sync, just a soft little plot.

The violets chimed in, with humor in tone,
"Who needs a throne when you've got your own zone?"
The thistles were shocked, as they tried to partake,
But tangled up badly, making all flowers quake.

As the sun set low, they reminisced in the lark,
In a garden of laughter, where wit left its mark.
With thorns and with blooms, each dance took the lead,
In this tale of the tangles, humor was freed!

Green Tapestry Tales

In a garden bright and cheery,
The daisies hold a chat, quite merry.
The tulips talk about their height,
While violets giggle with all their might.

A sunflower spins in a goofy dance,
As ants clumsily prance in a line, not a chance.
The roses blush, feeling quite fine,
While the weeds laugh on, 'We're just divine!'

Pansies wear frowns like a silly cap,
While squirrels plot a mischief map.
"Let's paint the fence, a vibrant hue!"
"Oh dear," says a petal, "What will they do?"

In this tapestry, laughter blooms loud,
A garden of giggles, a whimsical crowd.
With each frenzied whisper and laugh so spry,
Nature's vibrant jest fills the sky.

In the Company of Butterflies

A butterfly flits with outrageous flair,
Swapping secrets with bees like a pair.
"Did you see how I swooped just right?"
The ladybug laughs, "Oh what a sight!"

Caterpillars munch while telling tall tales,
Of moonlit dances and sailing on gales.
In the garden, snails ooze with grace,
Slowly shrugging, "We're winning this race!"

A moth joins in, with its fuzzy wing show,
"Life's a masquerade, do you want to glow?"
Together they swirl, a colorful crew,
Mixing up joy like a wild, vibrant stew.

And as the flowers join in with their cheer,
This whimsical party is the best of the year.
With laughter so bright, it's impossible to miss,
In nature's own gala, there's complete bliss.

Sculpting Life in Earthy Hues

In the rich brown earth, humor takes root,
Where mushrooms wear hats and dance in pursuit.
"Watch me twirl, I'm the king of the patch!"
The pinchy little frogs join up for a match.

The carrots debate if they're more like kings,
"They wear orange crowns and grow in strange rings!"
The peas joke, "Our pods are the best!"
While potatoes ponder their tuberous quest.

A hedgehog grins, winks at the sun,
"Let's throw a bash and see who can run!"
The worms will wiggle and sing loud and clear,
With laughter in dirt, there's never a fear.

In earthy tones, the laughter we weave,
Each critter a character, eager to thieve
A moment of joy from the everyday grind,
In this garden of quirky, we're all intertwined.

Mosaic of the Meadow

In a meadow mosaic, colors collide,
Where daisies and dandelions dance side by side.
A grasshopper hops, thinking it's grand,
While crickets sing tunes with a quirky band.

"I'm the best jumper!" a young bunny declares,
While chasing a squirrel that just doesn't care.
With flowers debating who's the brightest hue,
The air is alive with a challenge or two.

"Let's play hide and seek!" squeaks a young bee,
"Hiding in petals is where I'll be!"
The sunbeams chuckle, dappling the scene,
As shadows play tag, oh what a routine!

With each little giggle and playful cheer,
This meadow of magic brings everyone near.
So here's to the blooms and the laughter they share,
In this whimsical world, nothing can compare.

Nature's Palette of Grace

In gardens full of color bright,
A daisy danced, oh what a sight.
The roses laughed, the tulips cheered,
As bees in tiny suits appeared.

With every bloom, a joke is told,
The sunflowers bicker, bold and gold.
Violets chuckle, they're so small,
While orchids strut, they bloom, stood tall.

The daisies wink, with petals white,
Silly little bugs take flight.
Butterflies in tutus twirl,
In this wild, whimsical world.

So grab a pot and pluck a stem,
Join in the laughter, don't condemn.
Nature's jokes, they never tire,
In this lively floral choir.

A Stroll Through Scent

A whiff of mint, a dash of spice,
Roses sneezing, oh how nice!
Lilies giggle, so refined,
While dandelions blow, unconfined.

The jasmine hums a silly tune,
As daisies dance beneath the moon.
Lavender tosses soothing vibes,
But geraniums plot funny jibes.

Sunflowers, oh, they twist and pose,
Tickling each other's pointed toes.
Petunias wear hats made of dew,
Chasing breezes, how they flew!

So stroll along this fragrant lane,
Where even the weeds join in the game.
One sniff, and you'll be feeling great,
In this scented world, don't hesitate!

Song of the Snapdragon

Snapdragons snap, with quite a flair,
They chatter and gossip, if you dare.
Their colorful heads up in the air,
Whispering secrets, making quite a pair.

With petals that open wide with glee,
They giggle at the buzzing bee.
Oh, snapdragons, queens of the show,
With jokes that only flowers know.

They tease the roses, call them prudes,
And make the sunflowers change their moods.
In vibrant hues, they nap and play,
Creating a ruckus every day.

So come and listen to their lore,
As they giggle, oh, so much more.
In their garden theater, you will find,
The funniest show mankind's designed!

Sun-Kissed Blossoms

Sun-kissed flowers on a sunny morn,
Wear sunflower hats, all brightly worn.
Pansies joke with faces so sly,
While daisies flutter, oh my, oh my!

The tulips giggle, shaking their stems,
While marigolds greet you with gems.
"Oh look!" says one, "a bee in a hurry!"
He stumbles past, causing quite a flurry.

Lillies join in, their petals aglow,
Strutting around to steal the show.
Buttercups chuckle as they twirl,
In this vibrant dance, nature's swirl.

With sun above lighting each petal,
These blooms won't stop, oh, they won't settle.
In every garden, laughter's the key,
Join in the fun—it's a floral spree!

The Dance of Daisies

In a field where daisies twirl,
They giggle and spin, oh what a whirl!
With every breeze, they toss and sway,
They're having a ball, hip-hip-hooray!

The petals clap in cheerful cheer,
While ladybugs dance, no need to fear,
A butterfly joins, thinking it's grand,
Together they frolic, a merry band.

But watch out! Here comes a bumblebee,
Thinking he's king, buzzing with glee,
The daisies all chuckle, they won't let him win,
"Just stay in the flower crown, and spin!"

So if you see them in sunny array,
Just smile and join in their silly ballet,
In the dance of daisies, so light and spry,
You might just find your worries fly high!

Secrets of the Garden's Heart

In the garden where secrets thrive,
A gnome spills tales, oh what a dive!
He says the carrots are plotting a scheme,
To take over the world, or so it would seem.

The cucumbers whisper with leafy glee,
"Let's make a salad, just wait and see!"
While the onions hide, their eyes all a-well,
"Hold your horses; it's not time to tell!"

Amidst this chaos, the roses pout,
"Why do they always leave us out?"
With thorns they complain, "We're sharper than them,"
But secretly, they love their leafy mayhem.

So wander round, but keep your ears keen,
The garden's secrets are never routine,
With laughter and mischief all day long,
In this leafy world, you can't go wrong!

Blossom Whispers

The tulips gossip, their heads held high,
"Did you hear? The violets? Oh my, oh my!"
With colors bright and stories wild,
Each tale has a twist, like a giggling child.

The daffodils nod, with their sunny faces,
Sharing snippets of their secret places,
While the bees buzz in, all fuzzy and round,
Joining the chatter, what joy can be found!

A sunflower leans, with a towering height,
"Listen closely, hear the buds' delight!"
They share their dreams of the breezy night,
Of moonlit dances, oh, what a sight!

So if you pause in a garden so fair,
Listen for giggles riding the air,
Each blossom holds a story so sweet,
In whispers of joy, they tap dance on heat!

Radiance in the Underbrush

In the underbrush, where laughter grows,
A squirrel ties ribbons on all of his toes,
With acorn hats, they prance and twirl,
Turning the wild into a joyous whirl.

The mushrooms chuckle, all round and stout,
"Did you see Benny? He jumped right out!"
When raindrops fall, they splash and swing,
Making a ruckus like a lively spring.

A hedgehog appears, all spiky and bold,
Trading his quills for some tales to be told,
"Join our romp; don't just pine!
Let's dance past the roots, it'll be divine!"

So wander where wild things giggle in shade,
Find the radiance in the games they've made,
For joy festers deep in nooks and bends,
In underbrush laughter, where nature pretends!

The Colorful Canvas of Spring

In gardens bright with blooms so bold,
The flowers dance, a sight to behold.
Daisies wear hats, roses blush pink,
They gossip and giggle, what do you think?

A sunflower struts, tall and proud,
While tulips huddle, not so loud.
They joke about bees, zooming with flair,
Trying to catch a whiff of the air.

With every sprout, new stories to weave,
In leafy green coats, they trick and deceive.
A goofball weed, with roots o' so deep,
Swears he's a flower, but can't take the leap!

So come to the garden, enjoy the show,
Where petals are playful and chatter will flow.
A canvas bursting, a vivid array,
Spring's funny circus, come laugh the day away!

Lush Life's Serenade

In the warm embrace of tangled vines,
Plants serenade with quirky lines.
Cacti joke about their pointy plight,
While ferns flap their fronds in sheer delight.

A lazy lily in a pond takes a nap,
Swan boats float by, it's all a mishap.
And as the breeze sends whispers afloat,
Snapping-turtle joins in, wearing a coat!

Oh, dandelions puff with glee,
As children blow wishes, along with debris.
They laugh as they tickle the breeze with their fluff,
Only to find out, life's never enough!

Twists and turns in this leafy promenade,
A petunia hat party, a floral charade.
So join in the fun, it's a leafy affair,
Where laughter and petals fill up the air!

Echoes of the Meadow

In the meadow where the grass grows tall,
A chatter of insects, oh what a call!
Butterflies flutter with great aplomb,
While daisies nod, like they're in a prom.

A clumsy rabbit hops with no grace,
Chasing after shadows, in a wild race.
While squirrels throw acorns, can you believe?
It's a nutty dance, they never deceive!

The wind carries whispers, secrets untold,
With every flower a story unfolds.
"Oh look at that clover, so lucky and bright,
He's convinced he's a four-leaf, quite the sight!"

So gather around, let the giggles rise,
In this playful meadow, where laughter belies.
Every blade of grass is a stand-up star,
In the echoes of joy, we'll travel far!

A Symphony of Stems

In a patch of greens, where the stems all sway,
A beetle breaks out in a Broadway play.
Carrots sing bass while onions harmonize,
Making up tales of their veggie goodbyes.

Petunias waltz, with petals so bright,
While radishes grumble, feeling left out of sight.
"Oh dear tomato, you're quite the diva!"
Cheered by potatoes, basking in the fever.

And down by the roots, a party begins,
With earthworms wriggling to some funky spins.
"Join the jam, we're the underground crew,
Without us, dear plants, what would you do?"

As stripes of color intertwine in glee,
It's a symphonic garden, come laugh with me!
In this wacky world of vibrance and cheer,
Every root and petal spreads joy far and near!

The Secret Language of Buttercups

In the garden, whispers bloom,
Buttercups giggle, chase away gloom.
They dance in sunlight, oh so bright,
Telling secrets of pure delight.

Bees in tuxedos, buzzing with glee,
Trying to steal the show, oh dear me!
With nectar drinks, a sweet ballet,
Nature's humor on full display.

Bumbling bugs think they can sway,
But the flowers just grin and play.
A petal bash, a vibrant affair,
Stumbling blooms, without a care.

So next time you see a sprout,
Remember their laughter, hear them shout.
In a world where petals prance,
You'll find joy in every chance.

Dreams Woven in Green

In fields where daisies dream of flight,
They plot and plan through day and night.
With tangled roots and thoughts so grand,
They weave their wishes, hand in hand.

A squirrel cackles, stealing seeds,
While flowers giggle, fulfilling needs.
With petals bright, they form a scheme,
To turn the park into a team.

Underneath the shade of trees,
Lies a party with buzzing bees.
They prance and twirl, quite the show,
Chasing shadows, to and fro.

As twilight wanes, dreams take flight,
In a tapestry of jest and light.
Remember this tale of green and cheer,
Where laughter's magic draws us near.

Enchanted Oasis

In a patch of land where laughter flows,
A cactus tells jokes as the garden grows.
Laughter bubbles up like morning dew,
In this oasis, where whimsy is true.

The willows sway, throwing shade so wide,
While garden gnomes take a playful ride.
Wearing hats that are far too tall,
They pose like models, laughing through it all.

Goldfinches chirp in a comic tune,
As daisies compete for the best costume.
Colorful petals flaunt their style,
A flower dance, you'll want to stay awhile.

So come visit this patch of delight,
Where every bloom sparkles with light.
With jokes in the breeze and smiles afloat,
You'll leave with a giggle, that's the note!

The Emerald Embrace

In a meadow of mischief, grass tickles toes,
While mushrooms act shy, hiding their rows.
Lettuce lounges, feeling quite fab,
As the wind tells tales, oh what a gab!

Lilies in slippers, quite the parade,
With spinach in tuxedos, so well displayed.
A party of greens, both crunchy and fun,
Chasing sunshine, skipping on the run.

Petunias gossip about the next bloom,
Crafting shenanigans that fill up the room.
With every petal, they weave a joke,
As laughter and color in harmony spoke.

So next you wander where nature plays,
Join in the dance on these funny days.
In the emerald embrace of laughter's call,
Find joy in the petals, one and all.

Fragments of Fragrance

In the garden, a daisy wore a hat,
Said, "I'm fancy, look at that!"
A bumblebee buzzed with a grin,
"You look lovely, let the fun begin!"

But roses laughed, their petals bare,
"We are the stars, look at our flair!"
The daisies twirled, still feeling spry,
"We bloom in summer, oh my, oh my!"

A sunflower danced under the sun,
"Just join our party, it'll be fun!"
With sunshine smiles, they took to the breeze,
Forget the thorns, just be at ease!

So raise a glass of pollen cheer,
Let every flower spread good cheer!
In the garden, laughter's a boon,
With petals that sway, we'll dance till noon!

Enchantment in Evergreen

In the woods, where whispers flow,
A pine tree said, "I steal the show!"
With needles sharp and a knotted grin,
"I'm the king, let the fun begin!"

A squirrel chimed in, tail held high,
"You've got the height, but I can fly!"
With acorns tossed and laughter loud,
"Join our circus, come be proud!"

Moss joined in, wearing vibrant shoes,
"My green's the best, it's what I choose!"
From trunk to twig, they danced around,
In the evergreen, joy was found!

So sing with the leaves, let worries cease,
Under the branches, find your peace!
In laughter's arms, we all belong,
In the scents of pine, we sing our song!

Dance of the Tulips

At dawn, tulips put on a show,
In colors bright, they steal the glow!
"Look at me, I'm the best ballet,
With petals wide, I'll twirl away!"

A wind gust blew, gave them a shake,
"Hold on tight, for goodness' sake!"
They giggled soft, then did a flip,
In the morning sun, they took a dip!

Ladybugs joined with their polka dots,
"Let's boogie down, here's what we've got!"
Bouncing blooms with laughter in air,
In a crazy conga, they danced without care!

With friends all around, they spun in delight,
Life's a party from morning to night!
So when you see tulips, don't just stroll,
Join their dance, feel the joy in your soul!

Tales from the Trellis

On the trellis, grapes laughed with glee,
"We're fancy fruit, come sip with me!"
With vines all twisted, tales to tell,
"Join our party, we're under a spell!"

A butterfly floated, oh so fine,
"I'm here for nectar, you've got the wine!"
With winks and flutters, they shared a joke,
"Who knew that plants could make such smoke?"

Beans on a string were having a ball,
"We're climbing high, oh, what a haul!"
Together they laughed, with humor so spry,
Under the sun, with happy sighs!

So trek to the trellis, where joy blooms bright,
In the laughter of nature, everything's right!
With roots and shoots, let's raise a cheer,
For the funny tales we hold so dear!

Lurking in Leafy Shadows

In the garden, gnomes do peek,
Behind the leaves, they play hide and seek.
One's on a cabbage, what a sight!
Waving his hat, oh what a fright!

Rabbits chuckle, he's lost his way,
Dancing with daisies, come what may.
They tease him with carrots, just for fun,
Under the sun, the games have begun.

A sunflower giggles, "You look so small!"
The gnome pouts back, "I'm the life of the hall!"
But who can resist such leafy delight?
With petals as pillows, they party all night.

So if you wander, keep your head clear,
Watch for the ruckus, and lend an ear.
For in leafy shadows, the antics are true,
Where mischief blooms in every hue.

The Art of Blooming

Petals in yoga, stretching wide,
Sunbeams and giggles as plants collide.
A rose shouts, "Look at my tutu bloom!"
While daisies twirl, creating a room!

Bumblebees buzz with a beat so sly,
Wings with rhythm, oh my, oh my!
The orchids roll in, sophistication rare,
While tulips blush, caught in a flare.

Laughter erupts from the clover patch,
"Who knew we could make such a match?"
With winks and smiles, nature's parade,
Dancing in colors that never will fade.

So join the chorus of blossoms so free,
In this garden ballet, come laugh with me.
For every petal and leaf is a stage,
In the comedy of life, we engage.

Charms of the Canopy

Up high in the branches where the critters laugh,
Squirrels in tuxedos, doing their math.
Nuts in their pockets, they strut with flair,
Twisting and turning, without a care.

The owl with glasses, who thinks he's the wise,
Jokes with the woodpecker, who's poking for flies.
"Why did the tree not answer my call?"
"Because it was stumped!" echoes through the hall.

Vines start to swing, like ropes in a game,
As monkeys in hats join the wild acclaim.
What fun in the canopy, laughter takes flight,
Under the green roof, day turns to night.

So next time you wander right into a grove,
Listen for giggles, they're all in the know.
For charm in the canopy brings stories to share,
Where whimsy meets wisdom in the sweet, cool air.

Fragrance of Enchanted Paths

On the trail of scents, come whiff the delight,
Minty fresh giggles and roses so bright.
Lavender whispers a tale of fun,
While honeysuckle hums, "Oh, let's run!"

The mushrooms chuckle as squirrels trot by,
"Do we smell cake or is it just pie?"
While daisies dangle in curious knots,
Waving at passersby connecting the dots.

The breeze carries scents of wild raspberry,
A cheeky aroma, oh so merry.
With petals drifting like laughter in air,
Every step blooms with stories to share.

So trek through the pathways, let humor unfold,
In gardens of gleeful, fragrant gold.
For every sweet scent is a memory made,
In the dance of the petals, our joy displayed.

A Whirlwind of Wildflowers

In the garden, a dance of petals,
Bees in tutu, buzzing with wobbles.
Sunflowers giggle, oh what a sight,
Dandelions play tag, they take flight.

Tulips there, in a silly parade,
Waving their heads, in a colorful charade.
The marigolds chuckle, bringing delight,
While violets gossip, not shy, what a night!

Butterflies laugh, on a sugary spree,
Stealing the nectar, oh what a glee!
A breeze gives a twirl, oh the blooms sway,
Like a party of colors that come out to play.

A whirlwind of wildflowers at play,
With petals and pollen, they brighten the day!
In this chaos of colors, all laid bare,
Nature's own circus, without a care.

The Grace of Overgrown Corners

In the corner of the yard, what a scene!
Weeds doing ballet, so slick and so keen.
They pirouette past the old rusty chair,
While mushrooms gossip in a funky hair pair.

A rogue tomato, with a cheeky grin,
Hides from the rabbits, a champion of sin.
Dandelions poke fun at the lawn's bald spots,
While clovers unite in their knotty little plots.

The fence has a story, with vines intertwined,
A green tapestry, artfully designed.
Ladybugs dance, with grace so sincere,
In the messy patchwork, they bring up good cheer.

For in overgrown corners, life's a delight,
With whimsy and laughter all taking flight.
Nature here tickles, each petal and sprout,
A graceful ensemble, with joy all about.

Soft Brushstrokes of Nature

With a gentle touch, the painter arrives,
Creating a canvas where laughter thrives.
Strokes of green splashed on the earth's face,
Flecks of pink giggle but keep their pace.

A spotted toad hops, in the puddles they play,
While daisies wear crowns, enjoying the day.
Pinecones are juggling, with glee and finesse,
Nature's own clowns, in a colorful mess.

Clouds dribble colors like a child set free,
They plop on the flowers with quirky glee.
With soft brushstrokes, the day is alive,
A palette of joy where the critters thrive.

In this art gallery, life doesn't bore,
With fun colors splashed on the fern-laden floor.
Nature's own laughter paints every scene,
In soft brushstrokes, love's art is serene.

Whimsical Whispers in the Grove

In the heart of the grove, secrets unfold,
Mushrooms plot mischief, daring and bold.
Squirrels spin tales of acorn treasure,
While owls offer wisdom, wrapped up in leisure.

The willows are giggling, swaying with glee,
As a breeze tells jokes—oh, what can it be?
Beneath the big oaks, the rabbits conspire,
To throw the wildest tea party, oh, what a fire!

A parade of insects with hats quite absurd,
Strut their stuff, not one is deterred.
Fluttering leaves play, as whispers arise,
Of adventures uncharted beneath fuzzy skies.

In the grove, laughter blends with the sound,
Of whimsy and wonder, both lost and found.
Nature's embrace, with a wink and a smile,
Whispers of folly making hearts dance a mile.

www.ingramcontent.com/pod-product-compliance
Lightning Source LLC
Chambersburg PA
CBHW071815160426
43209CB00003B/94